NFL★TODAY

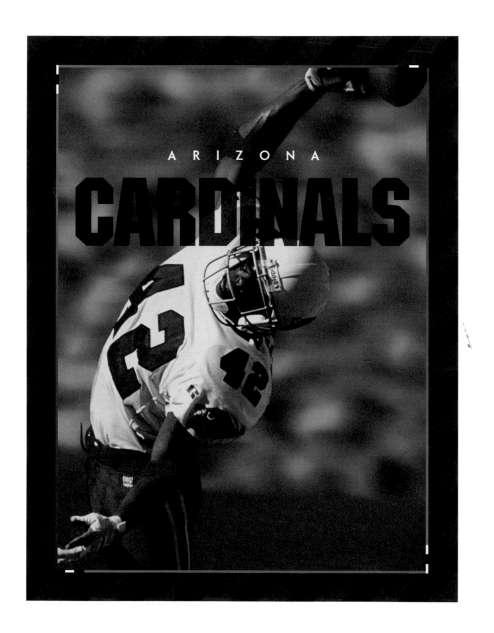

ARIZONA
CARDINALS

MICHAEL GOODMAN

CREATIVE ✿ EDUCATION

Published by Creative Education
123 South Broad Street, Mankato, Minnesota 56001
Creative Education is an imprint of The Creative Company

Designed by Rita Marshall
Cover illustration by Rob Day

Photos by: Allsport Photography, Associated Press, Bettmann Archive,
Duomo, Focus on Sports, Fotosport, and SportsChrome.

Library of Congress Cataloging-in-Publication Data

Goodman, Michael E.
Arizona Cardinals / by Michael Goodman.
p. cm. — (NFL Today)
Summary: Traces the history of the team from its beginnings through 1996.
ISBN 0-88682-807-4

1. Arizona Cardinals (Football team)—History—Juvenile literature.
[1. Arizona Cardinals (Football team) 2. Football—History.]
I. Title. II. Series.

GV956.A75G66   1996   96-15229
796.332'64'09791—dc20

123456

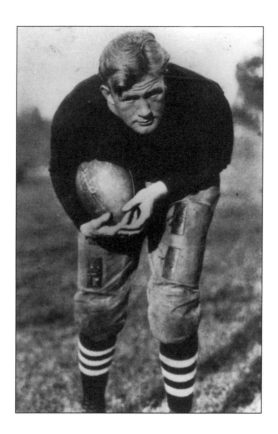

One of the early European settlers along Arizona's Salt River was an Englishman named Darrel Dupa. Noticing that the settlers were building a new town atop the ruins of an old Native American community, he recalled the legend of the phoenix, a mythical bird that burned up but then was reborn from its own ashes. So he called this new town Phoenix.

Over the years, Phoenix grew from a small town to a booming city. The area's dry, sunny climate, clean air and beautiful desert scenery lured tens of thousands of new residents—and one professional football team. In 1988, the St. Louis Cardinals franchise in the National Football League relocated

Ernie Nevers was a star at Stanford before joining the Cardinals.

1 9 2 1

"Paddy" Driscoll was not only a star player, he also coached the Cardinals in 1921-22.

in the Phoenix area, seeking to attract a new group of fans and hoping, like the phoenix, to achieve a rebirth of its old glory in the league.

"The Arizona Cardinals" is one of the newer team names in the NFL, but the team isn't new. In fact, it is the oldest professional football franchise in the United States, born long before the NFL was established. The team began play in Chicago back in 1899, then found its way to St. Louis in 1960 before heading out west in 1988.

While the club has won only two league championships over the years and has most often finished out of the playoffs, many Cardinals stars have earned their rightful places in NFL history. The Pro Football Hall of Fame has welcomed several former Cardinals greats, including Ernie Nevers, Paddy Driscoll, Charley Trippi, Ollie Matson, Larry Wilson and Jackie Smith. And Cardinals fans from Chicago to Arizona have a special place in their hearts for such past stars as quarterbacks Jim Hart, Neil Lomax and Paul Christman; running backs Ottis Anderson, Stump Mitchell, Terry Metcalf and John David Crow; and receivers Roy Green, Mel Gray and Ricky Proehl.

In the mid-1990s, Arizona fans have had some new heroes to cheer for—such as Rob Moore, Garrison Hearst and Larry Centers. If these talented players achieve their great potential, then Cardinals fans are in for a rebirth of exciting football in the Arizona desert.

A NORMAL START

The Arizona Cardinals franchise not only began its existence in a different city, it started with a different name, too. In

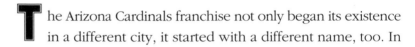

Larry Centers emerged as a rushing threat in the 1990s (page 7).

Player-coach Ernie Nevers led the Cardinals to a 5-6-2 record.

1899, a Chicago painter and builder named Chris O'Brien gathered several friends and family members together to form the Morgan Athletic Club. O'Brien later moved the club's home to Chicago's Normal Field, and everyone began calling the team the Normals. When O'Brien made a deal for some bright-red secondhand jerseys from the University of Chicago, he gave the team a new name, the Cardinals, to fit its new uniforms.

When the NFL was formed in the early 1920s, the Cardinals immediately became one of the league's top teams, thanks mainly to star player John "Paddy" Driscoll. Driscoll was an outstanding halfback on offense and cornerback on defense. He also dropkicked field goals with great accuracy and tripled as the team's head coach. Driscoll led the club to an 11-2-1 record in 1925 and its first NFL championship.

Unfortunately, the city of Chicago was in love with another local team—the Bears. As a result, attendance for Cardinals' games remained low, and the club's financial picture became bleak. O'Brien was forced to sell Driscoll to the Bears following the championship season, and then, after three straight losing seasons (1926–1928), he sold the entire franchise to a Chicago doctor named David Jones.

NEVERS NEVER QUITS

The Cardinals' new owner had a plan—a one-man plan— to make the team a winner. That man was Ernie Nevers, who had gained national fame as a bruising halfback at Stanford University. Before the 1929 season, Jones convinced the 6-foot 1, 210-pound Nevers to sign with the Cardinals as player-coach. Now his team had a star in Chicago exciting enough to steal the headlines from the Bears.

"People used to say I should try to avoid getting hit," Nevers recalled. "But that wasn't football to me. What it was all about was making a tackler know you were around. That's what football was meant for—contact. I guess I got the greatest satisfaction out of popping a lineman—you know, really laying into him and then going on to somebody else."

In his first season with the Cardinals, Nevers got a chance to show just how good he was, and, best of all, he did it against the Bears. "I don't need to tell you about Nevers," Bears' head coach George Halas told his players before the game between the Chicago rivals. "If you stop him, you stop the Cardinals." That was easier said than done. Here's how sportswriter Phil Berger described it: "Everybody in Comiskey Park the afternoon of November 28 knew what would happen. Very simply, Ernie Nevers would try to destroy the Bears by himself." He tried, and he did. The 8,000 fans stared in disbelief as Nevers dismantled the Bears' defense, scoring six touchdowns and four extra points—40 points altogether—in a 40-6 Cardinals romp. Nevers' remarkable one-game scoring performance has never been matched by any other NFL player.

Nevers was a winner, but the Cardinals weren't. He played for and coached the Cardinals through the 1931 season and then retired. A year later, David Jones decided to sell the team to Chicago businessman Charles W. Bidwill, Sr. for $50,000. The new owner didn't change the club's luck, though. From 1933 to 1946, the Cardinals never rose above fourth place in the Western Division.

In 1946, Bidwill made a move that would turn the team around. He rehired Jimmy Conzelman as coach. Conzelman had piloted the Cardinals through losing campaigns from 1940–42; this time Bidwill would give him plenty of talent to work with.

1 9 3 1

Ernie Nevers retired after a successful career with the Cardinals.

Ottis Anderson was a powerful runner for the Cardinals (pages 10-11).

Charlie Trippi ran for 690 yards and seven touchdowns to lead the Cardinals offense.

"I've got a dream," Conzelman told Chicago sportswriters. "You have to have horses in the backfield, otherwise you're a doormat. I want the greatest backfield in the league—the best passer and the best runners. When I have all of that going for me, I'll have the professional championship in my pocket."

Conzelman explained his plan to his team owner and guaranteed an NFL title if the right personnel were brought in. Bidwill agreed to spend the money needed to acquire Conzelman's "Dream Backfield," and the coach began his search. Conzelman brought together quarterback Paul Christman, halfbacks Elmer Angsman, Jr., and Marshall Goldberg and fullback Pat Harder in 1946. He completed the backfield a year later by drafting lightning-quick halfback Charlie Trippi from the University of Georgia and signing him to the richest contract in league history—$100,000 spread over four years.

The "Dream Backfield" led the Cardinals to a 9-3 record in 1947, good enough for the Western Division title ahead of the second-place Bears. In the 1947 NFL championship game, the Cardinals outscored the Philadelphia Eagles 28-21. Conzelman had kept his promise to his team owner, but Charles Bidwill wasn't around to see it. He had died during the 1947 season. The following year, the Cardinals won another division title with an 11-1 record, the best in team history, and again met the Eagles for the NFL title. This time, however, Philadelphia came out on top, 7-0.

Conzelman decided to step down after the 1948 season, and the Cards went into a tailspin. They slumped to third place in 1949 and then began a streak of six straight losing seasons (1950–1955) after the club was shifted to the NFL's Eastern Division. The one bright spot for Cardinals fans during those years was the play of running back Ollie Matson, a future Pro Football Hall of Famer.

Matson joined the Cardinals in 1952, after winning two track medals in the 1952 Summer Olympics in Helsinki, Finland. He quickly established himself as a triple-threat star—rushing, receiving and returning kicks. Unfortunately, Matson couldn't turn the team around by himself, though he tried. Before the 1959 season, the Cards traded Matson to the Los Angeles Rams and got nine players in return—though he was probably better than all nine put together.

The Cardinals were willing to give up Matson because they had two young halfbacks ready to take over the team's rushing and pass receiving duties. John David Crow, a former Heisman Trophy winner, was an outstanding runner, and Bobby Joe Conrad was an excellent pass catcher.

The two men got their chance to star, but not in Chicago. Before the 1960 season, the Bidwill family decided that the Cardinals were no longer going to play second-fiddle to the more popular Bears; after 60 years in Chicago, the team was moved to St. Louis.

The change of scenery improved the team's fortunes. Led by Crow, Conrad, wide receiver Sonny Randle and a fine young quarterback named Charley Johnson, the Cardinals began to move up the ladder in the NFL's Eastern Division. Crow quickly won over the St. Louis fans by gaining 1,071 yards his first year in Missouri, while Randle caught a league-leading 15 touchdown passes. Their heroics helped the Cardinals record their second winning season (6-5-1) in a decade.

By 1963, new coach Wally Lemm could also call on the offensive skills of fullback Bill "Thunder" Thornton and flanker Bob

1 9 6 0

Cardinals receiver Sonny Randle was named to the All-Pro NFL team for his outstanding play.

*Tight end Jackie
Smith was named to
the Pro Bowl team
for the fourth
straight season.*

Paremore, a world-class sprinter. He also added placekicker
Jim Bakken, who would go on to set franchise records for con-
secutive games played and points scored during a remarkable
17-year career in St. Louis. This gathering of talent helped the
Cardinals go 9-5 in 1963 and 9-3-2 in 1964.

For the next few years, the Cards alternated good and bad
seasons, but better days were ahead for St. Louis fans. Slowly
but surely, the Cards acquired the players who would produce
one of the most exciting offensive teams in the NFL during the
1970s.

HART AND GRAY MAKE AIR CORYELL FLY

The Cardinals' first new offensive star arrived in St. Louis
in 1966. He was a little-known player from a little-known
nearby college—Jim Hart from Southern Illinois-Carbondale.
Hart wasn't even drafted by an NFL team. The Cardinals acquired
him as a free agent and he wasn't expected to stick around
long. But Hart would play 18 seasons in St. Louis and set most
of the team's passing records before he retired.

Hart was himself surprised by his success. "When I first tried
out, back in 1966," he recalled, "I was just worried about getting a job. I couldn't even fathom playing before crowds this
big. I'd see 60,000 spectators, and I'd be put in awe."

Hart's leadership made a definite improvement in the St. Louis
offense, but he needed more help. That assistance began arriv-
ing in the 1971 draft, when the Cardinals picked Missouri wide
receiver Mel Gray, noted more for his talent on the running
track than on the football field. Many experts considered Gray
to be just a sprinter who wouldn't be able to hold onto the
ball when he was hit by tacklers.

"They said I couldn't catch the ball, that my hands were like

Jim Hart established himself as a leader in the 1970s.

Guard Conrad Dobler was named to the Pro Bowl in recognition of his fierce blocking style.

bricks," Gray said. But he fooled the experts. Using his blinding speed to get behind defenders, Gray quickly became one of the most dangerous deep threats in the league. He averaged nearly 30 yards a catch in his rookie year and had four long touchdown receptions. "Gray proved conclusively that speed and agility will beat weight and height anytime," wrote *Sports Illustrated* reporter Rick Telander.

Hart and Gray were joined in 1973 by halfback Terry Metcalf, who was exceptional as both a receiver and a runner and also stood out as a top kick returner. But the key to the offense may have been not the backfield, but the All-Pro linemen blocking for them—center Tom Banks, tackle Dan Dierdorf and guard Conrad Dobler. They gave Hart time to pass and Metcalf room to run. The linemen made it possible for new Cardinals coach Don Coryell to install a great passing offense in St. Louis, known around the league as "Air Coryell."

Air Coryell revved up in 1973 and by 1974 was in full gear. That year, St. Louis won its first seven games of the season, including a thrilling 31-28 win over the defending Eastern Division champion Dallas Cowboys. The key play in that game was an 80-yard touchdown strike to Mel Gray. "They were trying to play me one-on-one, and that made me smile," Gray reflected. "I guess maybe people will start taking us seriously now."

The three-point win over Dallas was typical of the 1974 season for the Cardinals. Every game that year was close—maybe a little too close sometimes for St. Louis fans, who started calling their team the "Cardiac Cardinals" because of all the heart-stopping finishes. "I guess if there's a way to make a game closer, we'll think of it," said Coryell.

Despite a late-season fade, the Cardinals finished 10-4 and

#76 Dan Dierdorf fights past his opponent.

Jim Hart was always a threat to throw a bomb.

won their first division title since 1947. Unfortunately, the team's long-awaited return to the playoffs was short-lived. The Minnesota Vikings sent them home early with a 30-14 loss in the first round.

St. Louis won another Eastern Division title in 1975 with an 11-3 record. Terry Metcalf had a remarkable year. He gained a total of 2,462 yards rushing, receiving and returning kickoffs and punts. This set an NFL record for all-purpose yardage. Running back Jim Otis also asserted himself that year, gaining 1,076 yards rushing to balance the Cardinals' air attack. But in the playoffs, St. Louis couldn't stop the running game of the Los Angeles Rams and lost 35-23 in the first round. Coryell's Cardiac Cardinals kept winning close ones in 1976, finishing 10-4, but two tough losses to the Washington Redskins cost the team a playoff berth.

The team's fortunes declined after that. Coryell was fired fol- lowing a 7-7 year in 1977. Metcalf left the team in 1978 fol- lowing a contract dispute. Even Mel Gray was starting to slow down. However, in the 1979 draft, the Cardinals found anoth- er speed burner who would eventually take his place as the team's long threat and added an outstanding runner as well— Roy Green and Ottis Anderson.

Roy Green came out of tiny Henderson State University in Arkansas, not exactly a hotbed of pro football talent. But Green proved to be something special. He was drafted as a corner- back and started his pro career on defense. He also returned kickoffs and tied an NFL record with a 106-yarder against Dallas in his rookie year.

Don Coryell holds the best Cardinals coaching record with 42-29-1.

But during the 1981 season, Cardinals coach Jim Hanifan asked Green to take on additional offensive duties as a wide receiv- er. "I just want you to go in and run by everybody," Hanifan told Green. Roy didn't know much about the Cardinals offense, but he didn't really have to. He was a secret weapon whose job was to go long as quickly as possible. "It didn't matter what they called in the huddle," Green laughed. "I knew what I was doing."

When Green caught a 60-yard bomb from Jim Hart in his first game on offense, the St. Louis secret was out. He continued to play both offense and defense throughout the 1981 season. He caught and intercepted passes in three different games, some- thing that had not been done by any NFL player since 1957. "The only thing that Roy hasn't done is tape our ankles," com- mented Dan Dierdorf. "Maybe a lot of guys could play both ways, but it's one thing to say you're able to and another to actually do it. In a game of gifted athletes, Roy is exceptional."

High-flying Roy Green.

While Green was the team's new star over the airways, Ottis Anderson was grinding out yardage on the ground and setting one team record after another. In 1979, the rookie runner from Miami bulled his way over defenders for 1,605 yards, which is still a club one-year rushing standard. In addition he recorded 1000+ yard seasons in 1980,1981,1983 and 1984 as well.

LOMAX BRINGS OFFENSE TO MAXIMUM EFFICIENCY

1 9 8 1

Cardinals running back Ottis Anderson rushed for 1,376 yards and nine touchdowns.

R oy Green and Ottis Anderson were not the only new faces on offense in St. Louis in the early 1980s. After a series of lopsided losses during the 1981 season, coach Hanifan decided to bench Jim Hart in favor of rookie Neil Lomax. Lomax, who had set records at Portland State University, where he doubled as quarterback and baseball pitcher, was confident he could do the job.

"I have always felt that I can complete a pass or strike out a batter. I have always wanted to be the dominant, the take-charge kind of guy. Every play, I go all out to execute the best that I can. That's what good players do."

In his first four games as a pro starter, Lomax led the Cardinals to four straight victories. Suddenly, the once-hopeless Cards were in contention for a playoff spot. But the team lost its last two games to finish at 7-9. The club did make the playoffs in the strike-shortened 1982 season, but fell far short of the Super Bowl with a first-round loss to the Green Bay Packers.

By 1983, Lomax and Green had become the best quarterback-receiver combination in the league, combining for 78 passes, 1,227 yards and a league-leading 14 touchdowns. Their explosiveness, combined with Ottis Anderson's power, helped the Cardinals achieve winning seasons in both 1983 and 1984.

23

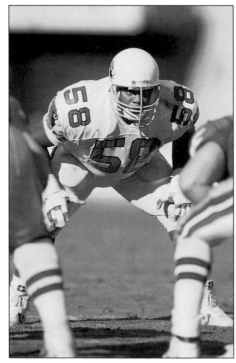

Left to right: J.T. Smith, Ron Wolfley, Eric Hill, Ken Harvey.

The team failed to qualify for the playoffs either year, but they came very close in 1984.

Going into the final game, St. Louis needed to beat the Washington Redskins to earn a post-season berth. The Redskins burst out to a 23-7 halftime lead and things looked pretty bleak. Then Lomax took charge in the second half, hitting Green for two touchdowns and setting up two Neil O'Donoghue field goals that brought the Cards within two points. With four seconds to go, O'Donoghue readied for a 50-yard field goal that would win the game. This time his kick fell inches short of the goal posts, and the Cardinals' season was over.

A year later, the Cardinals began to fall in the standings. The biggest problem was injuries. Lomax, Green and Anderson spent numerous games on the sidelines. During losing seasons in 1985, 1986 and 1987, St. Louis fans began to stay home, and team owner William Bidwill contemplated relocating the franchise once again.

In March 1988, Bidwill got permission from the league to take his team to Phoenix, and the club headed west looking to be reborn. Playing in Sun Devil Stadium in nearby Tempe, the Cards got off to a great start in 1988. They were 7-4 and seemed destined for a playoff berth. Neil Lomax, finally back from injuries, was having his best season ever, amassing over 3,400 yards passing in the first 11 games. J.T. Smith and Roy Green were each nearing 1,000 yards on receptions, and Earl Ferrell and Stump Mitchell were both solid rushing threats. But then Lomax began having trouble with his hip again and the club fell apart, losing its last five contests to finish a disappointing 7-9.

Things didn't get better in 1989. Lomax retired and coach Gene Stallings was fired following a 5-11 campaign. Bidwill brought

1 9 8 4

December 16: Neil Lomax set a club record with thirty-seven pass completions for 468 yards.

Ronald Moore led the Cardinals in rushing in 1993 (pages 26-27).

25

Running back Larry Centers established himself as a top scorer.

Things didn't get better in 1989. Lomax retired and coach Gene Stallings was fired following a 5-11 campaign. Bidwell brought in former Washington assistant coach Joe Bugel to turn the team around in 1990. Bugel built a new offense around quarterback Timm Rosenbach and two rookies, wide receiver Ricky Proehl and running back Johnny Johnson. Proehl topped all rookie receivers with 56 grabs, and Johnson made the Pro Bowl, but their efforts were not enough to overcome the Cardinals' woes on defense, which gave up a league-leading 50 touchdowns that year.

There was little improvement in the two seasons that followed. Before the 1993 season, Bidwell gave Bugel an ultimatum to produce a winning team this year or face the consequences. After a slow start, the club won five of its last eight games to end at 7-9. A close loss to the Giants on a last-second field goal kept the team below .500 and spelled Bugel's doom.

Yet the club had definitely improved under Bugel. Linebacker Eric Hill, the team's defensive captain, and lineman Eric Swann had established themselves as two of the league's top defenders; quarterback Steve Beuerlein directed a rejuvenated offensive attack featuring receivers Ricky Proehl, Randall Hill and Gary Clark; and rookie running back Garrison Hearst provided hope for a solid ground attack.

What the club needed was a dynamic new coach and general manager to shake things up a little. Bidwill knew the man he wanted—Buddy Ryan. Ryan had a checkered history. He was a defensive genius who had built up powerhouses in Chicago, Philadelphia and Houston. But he didn't always get along well with his players, fellow coaches or owners. As a result, Ryan often found himself looking for a new job. Now he was in Arizona, where he announced at his opening press conference, "You've got a winner in town."

Defensive tackle Eric Swann became a feared pass rusher.

Garrison Hearst led the team in rushing in 1995.

Linebacker Jamir Miller readies for action.

Veteran Boomer Esiason brings his aerial show to the Cardinals.

Ryan immediately began dealing and reorganizing to back up his boast. He brought in three All-Pros from his former teams—Seth Joyner, Clyde Simmons and Wilber Marshall—to bolster the Cards defense. He gave defensive back Aeneas Williams more responsibility in the secondary, and the young star responded by leading the league in interceptions and earning a Pro Bowl berth. He made versatile fullback Larry Centers his third-down specialist, and Centers became the Cards' newest offensive weapon.

Ryan's "new" Cardinals got off to a slow start in 1994 but by mid-season they emerged as the league's hottest team. The club finished the year at 8-8, just missing the playoffs with a tough last-game loss to Atlanta. The team's heart was clearly its defense, which gave up just 45 points in the fourth quarter all year long.

With the defense looking solid, Ryan focused on strengthening the offense in the 1995 season. Despite Ryan's efforts, the team went through major breakdowns in 1995, finishing last in the division at 4-12. Hearst gained more than 1,000 yards rushing, and Centers set a new club record with 101 pass receptions. But their efforts were just not enough. Arizona fans were very disappointed, and so was the team's ownership. Buddy Ryan was sent packing.

The Cardinals are rebuilding again. Fans hope that the club that originated in the midwest and that was reborn in Phoenix will someday bring a Super Bowl championship to its western home.